MEGALODON

AND OTHER PREHISTORIC MONSTERS OF THE DEEP

BY BRENDA GURR
ILLUSTRATED BY R.J. PALMER

becker&mayer!

CONTENTS

FROM PLANTLIKE TO PREDATOR

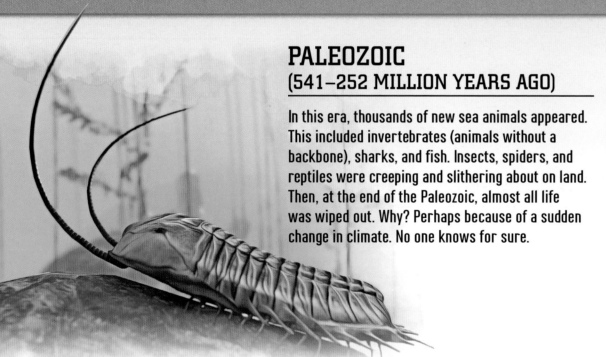

About 640 million years ago, the first animals appeared on Earth. They lived in the sea and were more like plants than animals. In fact, you could have swum right up to them and not realized they were animals at all! They looked more like a sea sponge. They had no brains, eyes, or mouths. They were silent and couldn't move. They probably weren't a lot of fun at parties.

Let's zoom ahead two hundred million years. Now you would be hopping out of the water right away! The sea animals during this time had not only brains and eyes—many had mouths full of teeth as well! These were enormous, seriously scary predators. They terrorized the oceans for millions of years.

The sea predators in this book lived in three eras: the Paleozoic, the Mesozoic, and the Cenozoic.

PALEOZOIC
(541–252 MILLION YEARS AGO)

In this era, thousands of new sea animals appeared. This included invertebrates (animals without a backbone), sharks, and fish. Insects, spiders, and reptiles were creeping and slithering about on land. Then, at the end of the Paleozoic, almost all life was wiped out. Why? Perhaps because of a sudden change in climate. No one knows for sure.

MESOZOIC
(252–66 MILLION YEARS AGO)

The first dinosaurs and sea reptiles appeared in the Mesozoic era—and ruled the planet! Scientists think this era ended with a gigantic asteroid crashing into Earth. This killed all giant dinosaurs and sea reptiles. Animals such as small birds, amphibians, and mammals survived.

541–252 MILLION YEARS AGO

DUNKLEOSTEUS

STETHACANTHUS

CLADOSELACHE

252–66 MILLION YEARS AGO

TEMNODONTOSAURUS

LIOPLEURODON

KRONOSAURUS

CENOZOIC
(66 MILLION YEARS AGO—PRESENT)

Truly enormous mammals lived in this era. Some were massive versions of animals we know today, such as rabbits and pigs. These not-so-cuddly creatures shared the planet with birds, insects, and the first humans. Sharks were the top predators in the sea.

FOSSILS ROCK!

How do we know that prehistoric predators existed? Because of fossils. Fossils are the remains of plants and animals that died thousands or even millions of years ago. They are usually found in rock. Fossils can tell scientists all sorts of things: where an animal lived, what it ate, how it moved, how big it was, and what other animals are related to it.

Animal fossils usually form from teeth, shell, or bone. These hard bits make the best fossils. A fossil can also be something an animal has created—footprints, tooth marks, and even poop have been fossilized! Not every animal or animal creation becomes a fossil. A fossil is only formed when these things have been quickly buried by layers of mud or sand.

FAST FACT

Sea fossils are often found on land. This can be because prehistoric seas have dried up over time. It can also be because the Earth's crust has been shifting. These shifts can be so huge that sea animal fossils have even been found on mountain tops!

66 MILLION YEARS AGO—PRESENT

ELASMOSAURUS

TYLOSAURUS

MOSASAURUS

BASILOSAURUS

MEGALODON

LIVYATAN

MESOZOIC [CONTINUED]

CENOZOIC

MEGALODON

SHARK KING!

Megalodon [MEG-uh-luh-dawn] comes from Greek words meaning "big tooth." But its teeth certainly weren't the only big thing about this super predator. It was almost three times the length of the great white shark—the largest shark alive today. *Megalodon* even makes *Tyrannosaurus rex* look puny. *T. rex* weighed about the same as an African male elephant. But experts think that *Megalodon* might have weighed about the same as *ten* elephants!

MEGALODON
52—59 feet (15.8—18 m)

COAST GUARD LIFEBOAT
47 feet (14.3 m)

For around seventeen million years, the mighty *Megalodon* lurked alongside dolphins, sea lions, fish, whales, and many other sea animals. It was most likely an apex predator—an animal that has no natural predators within its ecosystem. *Megalodon* had a bite that could have easily crushed a car, so it's not surprising no animals would have threatened its throne!

RIP MEGALODON

FAST FACT

Megalodon became extinct around two million years ago. Scientists think this was because too much of its prey vanished over time.

TORPEDO WITH JAWS

Megalodon was fast and torpedo-like—it could zoom through the water at around 12 miles (20 km) per hour. Experts believe it attacked whales by biting off their fins or tails so they couldn't swim away. It probably attacked smaller prey by shaking them to pieces or crushing them to death with its massive jaws. These jaws could open about 8 feet (2.4 m) wide. That's more than enough to swallow a person whole!

A MOUTHFUL OF KNIVES...

Megalodon had a giant mouth that extended past its eyes. Inside were triangular, razor-sharp teeth. Each tooth had serrated sides—like the cutting edge of a steak knife. These powerful weapons could slice through flesh or even bone in a single bite. *Megalodon* probably had about 250 teeth in its mouth. Imagine the cost of dental visits!

Like modern sharks, *Megalodon* probably broke and lost its teeth constantly. That's what comes from chomping through bone! But losing teeth isn't a big problem for sharks. They have rows of replacement teeth at the ready. When a tooth falls out, the tooth in the row behind moves forward to replace it, on a type of skin conveyer belt. Scientists think that *Megalodon* may have had about five rows of teeth. It probably lost thousands of teeth in its lifetime.

SEAFOOD DINNER—WITH A SIDE OF ROTTING MEAT?

Megalodon's favorite snacks seem to have been whale and dolphin. It also liked to munch on giant sea turtles, dugongs, large fish, and even other sharks. Now that's some seafood diet! While it was an expert killer, it may have also eaten dead animals that it came across. It seems it wasn't a fussy eater.

Scientists can work out what *Megalodon* ate because they have found bite marks that match its teeth in the fossil bones of different sea animals. *Megalodon* teeth are also found in fossil sites near the bones of whales and dolphins.

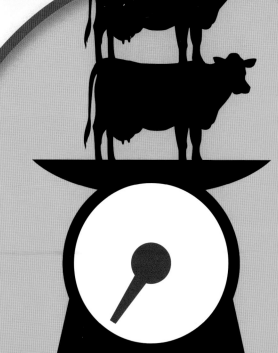

5 inches (12.7 cm)

Most *Megalodon* teeth that have been found are around 5 inches (12.7 cm) long. The biggest teeth found are about 7 inches (17.8 cm) long, which is the size of a man's hand. The largest tooth of a great white shark is less than half that size.

? KNOW WHAT?

Based on its giant size, scientists think that *Megalodon* needed to eat about 2,500 pounds (1,100 kg) of food per day. That's the weight of about two dairy cows!

MEGA REMAINS

Like all sharks, Megalodon had a skeleton that was mostly made up of cartilage—that's the bendy stuff in the tip of your nose and outer ear. Because cartilage is soft, it doesn't fossilize as well as bone. So a Megalodon skeleton has never been found. But what have been found are thousands of Megalodon teeth and some of its spine bones, or vertebrae. These have come from all over the world, from North and South America, to Europe, Africa, Asia, and Australia.

The most complete *Megalodon* vertebral column was found in Belgium in 1926. It is made up of 150 bones.

KNOW WHAT?
Hundreds of years ago, people thought *Megalodon* teeth were moon rocks or dragon tongues! It was not until 1666 that a scientist worked out what they really were.

MY NAME IS...

Since the 1800s, shark scientists have been arguing about whether *Megalodon* was closely related to the great white shark. Many thought it was and so most pictures you see of *Megalodon* look a lot like the great white. But recent research suggests that the two sharks may not have been close family. So, the scientific name of *Megalodon* has (for now) been changed from *Carcharodon megalodon* to *Carcharocles megalodon*. Does this mean *Megalodon* didn't look like the great white shark after all? Maybe not. Some scientists think it may have looked more like a super-size version of another modern shark, the sand tiger shark.

SAND TIGER SHARK

KNOW WHAT?
Famous fossil hunter Vito Bertucci, known as the "*Megalodon* Man," was so fascinated by *Megalodon* that he took almost twenty years to make a model of its jaw—which is about 11 feet (4 m) wide and 9 feet (2.7 m) tall.

MEET MEG'S FEROCIOUS FAMILY

Sharks are a type of fish that has been cruising the world's oceans for almost 420 million years. This makes them one of the most successful animal species ever. They were alive long before the dinosaurs appeared on Earth.

OTHER EARLY SHARKS

1. *ELEGESTOLEPIS*
[ELE-GES-TO-LEP-ISS]

Elegestolepis was the earliest known prehistoric shark. What did it look like? Well, this is a fishy mystery! We don't know much about it because it left only fossilized scales behind. It's because of these scales that we know sharks existed before any life on land.

2. *LEONODUS*
[LEE-ON-OH-DUS]

Leonodus lived about 380 million years ago. Scientists think it might have been about 16 inches (40.6 cm) long. When scientists first found *Leonodus* fossil teeth, they looked a lot like teeth from another type of prehistoric shark, *Xenacanthus*. This clue caused scientists to speculate that *Leonodus* may have been one of the rare prehistoric freshwater sharks, too.

KNOW WHAT?
Some prehistoric sharks ate only plankton—tiny plants and animals that drift with the ocean's currents. Some modern sharks are also planktivores. They include the megamouth shark, the basking shark, and the whale shark, which is the world's biggest living shark.

BASKING SHARK

SCARY, SCALY, SPINY, AND SNAKY

If someone says the word "shark," what springs to your mind? Perhaps a huge, gray, scary predator with lots of pointy teeth. But since ancient times, sharks have come in all shapes and sizes. And prehistoric sharks win the award for strangeness! Some had long snouts. Others had flippers that looked like wings.

Falcatus [fal-CA-tus] was only about as long as a pencil!

Hybodus [HI-bode-us] had many blunt teeth and a long spike sticking up on its back.

HYBODUS

FALCATUS

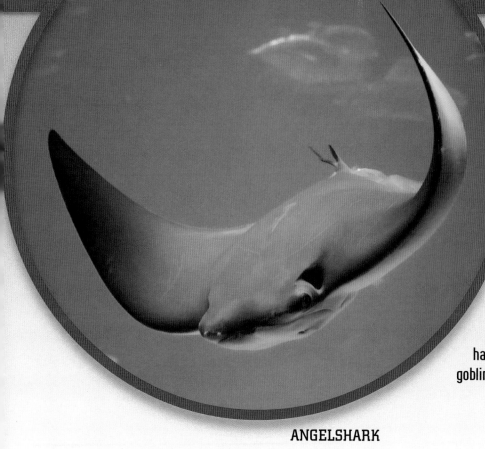

THESE ARE ... SHARKS?

Today there are still plenty of weird-looking sharks out there. You might already know of the hammerhead shark, but there are also sharks that look more like stingrays (angelsharks) or that have snake-like heads (frilled sharks.) There's also the sawshark, which has a snout with teeth sticking out of it, and the goblin shark, whose jaws can extend to catch its prey.

ANGELSHARK

SAWSHARK

LIVING FOSSILS

Sharks are sometimes called "living fossils"—animals that haven't changed a lot from their prehistoric forms. While this isn't strictly true, living sharks do have some things in common with their more recent prehistoric cousins. Both have tooth-like scales called denticles and skeletons made out of cartilage instead of bone. Cartilage is bendy but tough and lighter than bone. This means a shark can often outswim its prey. Unfortunately, cartilage doesn't fossilize well, so there are very few remains of prehistoric shark skeletons. It is lucky for us that sharks are always losing and replacing their teeth. Most of what we know about prehistoric sharks comes from tooth fossils.

KNOW WHAT?

When the fossil of a 380-million-year-old shark was found in Australia in 2005, scientists were startled. Not only was the fossil almost complete, but parts of the skeleton contained bones. It seems that early sharks may have started out with some bony bits and evolved their cartilage skeletons over time.

DEVONIAN-ERA SHARK

MEET FUNK TAIL, SHARP NOSE, AND IRONING BOARD

Looking kinda weird: The strangest prehistoric sharks

CRETOXYRHINA

100—80 million years ago

Scientists know a lot more about *Cretoxyrhina* [creh-TOX-ee-RYEE-nah] than they do about most prehistoric sharks because of some amazing fossil finds. Apart from teeth, nearly complete skeletons have been found, as well as skin impressions. These have denticles (scales) still intact! The most complete skeleton found so far was discovered in Kansas in 1890.

Cretoxyrhina was the largest shark of its time and preyed on a number of different sea creatures. This included the giant bony fish *Xiphactinus* [zye-FAC-tee-nus], which was no pushover itself! Scientists have even found *Cretoxyrhina* teeth embedded in the remains of a mosasaur, a huge sea reptile. And these were some teeth! They were smooth and tough and about 2—3 inches (5.1—7.6 cm) long. They were also very sharp. Because of these teeth, *Cretoxyrhina* has been nicknamed the Ginsu shark, after a brand of kitchen knives that are said to be able to cut through tin cans.

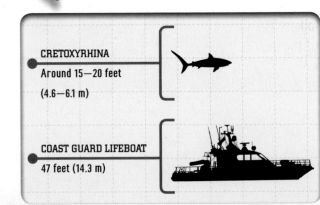

CRETOXYRHINA
Around 15—20 feet
(4.6—6.1 m)

COAST GUARD LIFEBOAT
47 feet (14.3 m)

STETHACANTHUS

370–345 million years ago

Stethacanthus [STETH-ah-KAN-thus] once swam in the shallows of the seas, where it ate small fish and shellfish. Its remains have been found in Europe, Asia, and North America. This is one of the strangest-looking of all prehistoric sharks. The male *Stethacanthus* had a weirdly shaped fin on top of its body—it looks like an ironing board topped with small spikes! This is a puzzle to scientists. Some think the freaky fin might have been used to show off the shark's strength to female sharks or to make it seem bigger. *Stethacanthus* also had spikes on its head. These might have helped to scare off predators. And last but not least, *Stethacanthus* had two long mysterious "whips" on its side fins.

STETHACANTUS	
2.3—6.5 feet	
(0.7 m to 2 m)	

COAST GUARD LIFEBOAT	
47 feet (14.3 m)	

CLADOSELACHE

375 million years ago

Cladoselache [KLAY-doh-SEL-ah-kee] was an early type of shark that has only been found in North America. It would have been a fast swimmer thanks to its slim body, large fins, and powerful forked tail. Some fossil remains of this shark have been found with prey still in its stomach! These remains tell us that *Cladoselache* swallowed its prey whole, tail first. Even though this shark had plenty of teeth, they were better designed for grabbing than ripping. Unlike modern sharks, *Cladoselache* wasn't covered in scales. It only had them around its mouth, eyes, and fins.

CLADOSELACHE	
6 feet (2 m)	

COAST GUARD LIFEBOAT	
47 feet (14.3 m)	

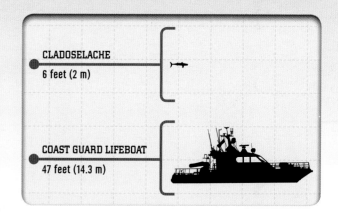

KNOW WHAT?
Until recently, the bizarre prehistoric predator *Helicoprion* [hel-ih-KOPE-ree-on] was thought to be a shark. But now scientists think it belongs to the shark-like chimaera family. *Helicoprion's* lower jaw teeth grew in a kind of spiral disc. Scientists aren't really sure why!

DUNKLEOSTEUS

BIG BONY BEAST

Dunkleosteus [dun-kel-OSS-tee-us] was a kind of prehistoric fish called a placoderm, which means "plate-skin." The elephant-sized *Dunkleosteus* appeared in the Devonian Period (also known as the Age of Fish) and was the largest animal of its time. Its remains were first discovered in 1867 in Ohio. It was named after Dr. David Dunkle, a scientist and former curator at the Cleveland Museum of Natural History. (The "-osteus" part means "bone.")

DUNKLEOSTEUS
Up to 33 feet (10 m)

COAST GUARD LIFEBOAT
47 feet (14.3 m)

PROTECTIVE ARMOR

Like all placoderms, *Dunkleosteus* had protective bony armor on its head and neck. This could be up to 3 inches (7.6 cm) thick. It even had a bony ring around its eye! So that's the front end . . . what about the rest? Well, unfortunately, fossil hunters have found only head and neck remains of *Dunkleosteus* so far. They have had to guess what the rest of the fish might have looked like based on fossils of smaller placoderms.

FAST FACT

A recent fossil find has shown that placoderms had something no living fish has—a set of stomach muscles, or abs! And they didn't even work out at the gym! Scientists think that the abs might have been used to steady a placoderm's body while it swam.

TOOTHLESS (BUT RUTHLESS)

You would think that such a huge predator would have huge teeth to match, right? Wrong. *Dunkleosteus* had no teeth at all! Instead, it had jaw blades with jagged edges like fangs. These could slice its prey into pieces. As the jaw opened and closed, the jagged edges rubbed against each other. This kept them nice and sharp all the time.

SUCKING JAWS OF DEATH

Dunkleosteus had an impressive skill. It could open and close its enormous jaws in a fraction of a second. This was so fast that it created a vacuum that pulled its prey (along with plenty of water) into its mouth. So it didn't need to get up close to its prey to grab it. It could just suck it up from a distance. This was handy because *Dunkleosteus* was very heavy. With all that armor, it wasn't built for speed.

Dunkleosteus had an amazingly powerful bite force. At the tip of its mouth, its bite may have matched that of a *T. rex*! It would have easily out-chomped any modern sharks.

Dunkleosteus could eat whatever it liked. But fossils show that younger ones usually went after softer prey like small sharks or bony fish. Adult *Dunkleosteus*, with their bigger, stronger jaws, seem to have tackled other placoderms.

MEET OTHER PLACODERMS

1. *TITANICHTHYS*
[TI-TAN-ICK-THISS]

This was another giant placoderm which grew almost as large as *Dunkleosteus*. But it was nowhere near as scary! Its jaw plates weren't sharp at all. They didn't need to be. This fish ate either very small fish or plankton.

2. *ROLFOSTEUS*
[ROLL-FOSS-TEE-US]

This placoderm was tiny—only about 6 inches (15 cm) long. It had a long snout that looked like a horn. Scientists aren't sure what this was used for, but it may have meant this fish had an excellent sense of smell.

KNOW WHAT?
Dunkleosteus fossils have been found with partially eaten remains of fish nearby. It seems that *Dunkleosteus* threw up bits it didn't like, including the bones. What terrible table manners!

TEMNODONTOSAURUS

DOLPHIN, FISH, OR . . . ?

If you had to guess what animal *Temnodontosaurus* [tem-no-DAWN-tuh-SAWR-us] was related to, what would be your first guess? A dolphin, perhaps? Nope. This Jurassic predator was not a mammal. What about a fish? No again. *Temnodontosaurus* was actually a type of large ichthyosaur—a sea reptile. Its name means "cutting-tooth lizard."

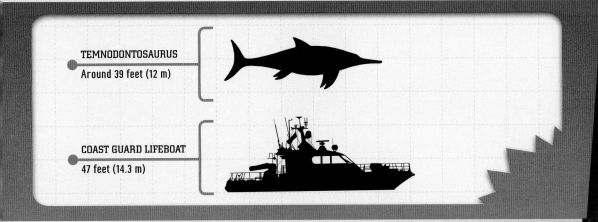

TEMNODONTOSAURUS
Around 39 feet (12 m)

COAST GUARD LIFEBOAT
47 feet (14.3 m)

FROM LIZARD TO FISH

You might be thinking that *Temnodontosaurus* looks nothing like a lizard. But its ancestors were land-dwelling reptiles. They may have been lizards or snakes. In fact, some of the earlier ichthyosaurs looked exactly like lizards with fins. Over time, they became more fish-shaped.

FAST FACT

The first ichthyosaurs appeared in the Triassic period, about 250 million years ago. The last ones disappeared in the Cretaceous, long before the dinosaurs became extinct.

SHE SELLS FOSSILS . . .

The first ichthyosaur skull ever found was of *Temnodontosaurus*. It was discovered in 1810 at the beaches of Lyme Regis, England, by a teenager named Joseph Anning. His twelve-year-old sister, Mary Anning, found the rest of the matching skeleton soon after. Mary became an important fossil collector and paleontologist. She often sold fossils and shells to make money for her poor family. Some people say she was the subject of the tongue twister "She sells seashells by the seashore."

Temnodontosaurus hunted in deep water for its prey. Not many animals do this because it is too dark to see much. But this wasn't a problem for *Temnodontosaurus*. It had gigantic eyes that let in lots of light. Its eyes are thought to be the largest eyes of any animal—ever. They were almost the size of dinner plates!

TOP SPEED PREDATOR

Temnodontosaurus was well suited to life in the water. It had a sleek and flexible body, a pointed snout, and four paddle-like flippers. All of these things meant it could swim at top speed. Scientists think it might have moved through the water by swishing its powerful tail from side to side. The only feature it didn't have to make a watery life easier was gills. *Temnodontosaurus* had to go to the surface to breathe air.

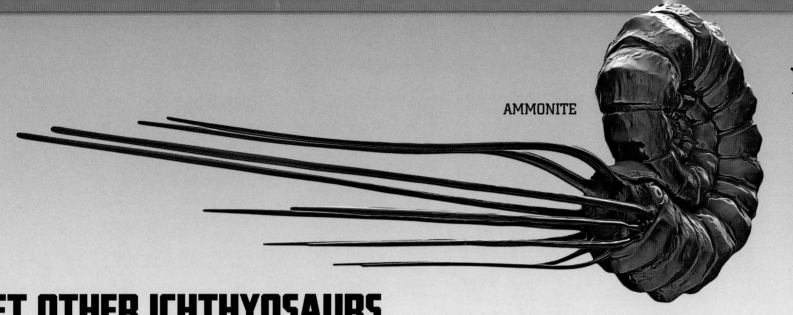

AMMONITE

YUMMY SQUID

Temnodontosaurus ate prey like fish and ammonites (a type of shelled animal closely related to squid.) It could easily crush an ammonite's shell with its sharp, strong teeth. It may have also eaten other small sea reptiles.

MEET OTHER ICHTHYOSAURS

1. *SHONISAURUS*
[SHOW-NEE-SAWR-US]

Shonisaurus looked a bit more like a whale than a dolphin. It was around 50 feet (15.2 m) long. Only the young had teeth, which were at the end of their snouts.

2. *SHASTASAURUS*
[SHAS-TAH-SAWR-US]

Shastasaurus has recently been named the largest marine reptile that has ever been found. It was about 68 feet (20 m) long! It didnt' have any teeth, so it only ate very soft prey.

1

2

?

KNOW WHAT?
Almost all modern reptiles lay eggs, but *Temnodontosaurus* gave birth to live young.

BABY CROCODILE HATCHES FROM EGG

ELASMOSAURUS

MOVE OVER, GIRAFFE!

Think a giraffe's neck is long? This Cretaceous plesiosaur beats it by miles. Its neck was about three to four times the length of an adult giraffe's! It made up about half of its body length and contained more than seventy bones. Though *Elasmosaurus* [eh-laz-mo-SAWR-us] is the long-neck record holder, its name doesn't have anything to do with necks. It means "thin plate lizard," and refers to its flat, thin hip bones.

ELASMOSAURUS
Up to 45 feet (14 m)

COAST GUARD LIFEBOAT
47 feet (14.3 m)

THE HEAD BONE'S CONNECTED TO THE ...TAIL BONE?

In 1869, scientist Edward Drinker Cope put the bones of an *Elasmosaurus* together. But he made a big mistake. He attached the head to the tail! Pictures of this were published in a scientific journal. When Cope realized his mistake, he tried to buy all the copies of the journal. Unfortunately, it was too late!

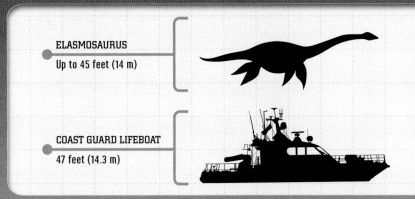

FAST FACT

Scientists still aren't sure how *Elasmosaurus* surfaced to breathe—its neck was so heavy, it probably couldn't lift its head out of the water. It's still a mystery.

MORE THAN JUST A NELK

Aside from a long neck, Elasmosaurus had some other interesting features.

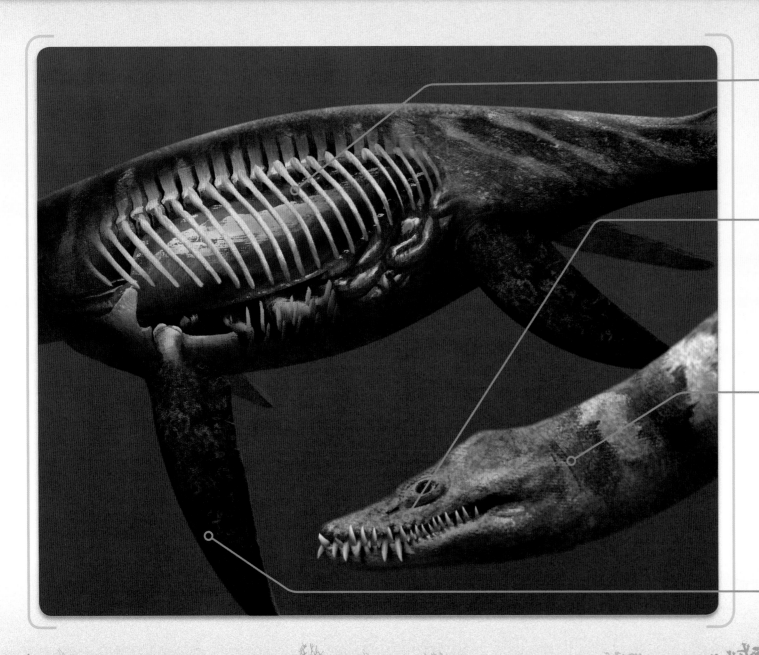

IT HAD ENORMOUS LUNGS

Like all reptiles, *Elasmosaurus* had to come to the surface to breathe air. But its lungs were so huge, it could have held its breath for a long time, perhaps for ten or twenty minutes.

IT HAD POINTY, OVERLAPPING TEETH

When its mouth was closed, its teeth acted like a trap. It could then swallow its prey whole.

IT HAD A VERY SMALL HEAD ON ITS LONG NECK

It was once thought that *Elasmosaurus* swam on the surface and snaked its head downwards to catch prey. But scientists now think it swam deeper underwater and stretched up to snatch its fishy snacks. This was ideal, as the small head wouldn't have looked too scary. If its prey didn't look too far beyond it, that is ...

IT FLEW UNDERWATER

Elasmosaurus was probably a graceful, slow swimmer. The latest research suggests it probably swam much like a penguin, using its two front flippers to "fly" through the water. Its back flippers were used for steering.

LOCH NESS
ELASMOSAURUS?

Is the Loch Ness monster real? Some people believe so. And if it is, they think it might be an *Elasmosaurus*. But scientists say this is unlikely. The loch is way too cold for our reptile friend. It also wouldn't contain enough food.

THE LOCH NESS MONSTER

MEET OTHER PLESIOSAURS

1. *PLESIOSAURUS*
[PLEE-ZEE-UH-SAWR-US]

This plesiosaur was around a long time before *Elasmosaurus*—it lived about 200 million years ago! Experts believe it caught prey by swinging its neck from side to side.

2. *THALASSOMEDON*
[THAL-AS-OH-MED-ON]

Almost as big as *Elasmosaurus*, this plesiosaur lived in North America. Its name means "sea lord" in ancient Greek.

KNOW WHAT?
Scientists have found round stones (gastroliths) in the stomachs of *Elasmosaurus* fossils. These might have been eaten to help grind up food in their stomachs.

KRONOSAURUS

NASTY NAMESAKE

Kronosaurus [KRONE-oh-SAWR-us] is a pliosaur named after Kronos, a thoroughly nasty ancient Greek god who swallowed all of his children. (Don't worry, they turned out fine.) *Kronosaurus* might have had a go at eating his own kids too.

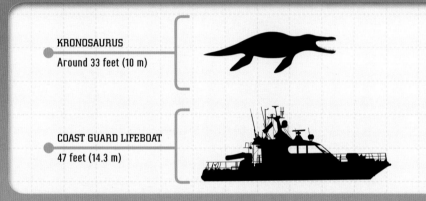

KRONOSAURUS
Around 33 feet (10 m)

COAST GUARD LIFEBOAT
47 feet (14.3 m)

CROC-LIKE KRONO

Kronosaurus looked a little like a crocodile, but it was actually one of the largest pliosaurs in the Cretaceous period of the Mesozoic era. This mega-reptile ate a range of prey, from large fish and turtles to squid and other giant sea reptiles. Two species of *Kronosaurus* have been found so far—one in Colombia and one in Australia.

FAST FACT

The heads of pliosaurs are huge compared to their body size. So scientists once thought that *Kronosaurus* was much longer than it really was. *Kronosaurus*'s head was about 6.5 feet (2 m) long. That's the length of a bed!

THAT CRUSHING FEELING

This sea monster had a jaw that could open extremely wide. Its mouth was lined with cone-shaped teeth. They weren't particularly sharp—but boy, could they crush! A turtle shell would have been no trouble for this awesome predator. The biggest *Kronosaurus* teeth that have been found are almost 12 inches (30 cm) long.

12 inches
(30 cm)

Kronosaurus also had four flippers that were like powerful paddles. It used all four to propel itself through the water. Scientists think it might have been super speedy over long distances.

FOSSIL FINDS

In 1930, an amazing *Kronosaurus* find was made in Queensland, Australia—a skull and a nearly complete skeleton. They were taken to Harvard University and put on display in Harvard's Museum of Natural History. But there is a small (actually, big) problem with the display. It is about 9.8 feet (3 m) longer than it ought to be! The scientists that created it gave it a few too many vertebrae. The bones were coated in plaster, so the display is sometimes called by the nickname Plasterosaurus.

KRONOSAURUS SKULL IN HARVARD MUSEUM OF NATURAL HISTORY

MEET OTHER PLIOSAURS

1. *PLIOSAURUS FUNKEI*
[PLY-oh-SAWR-us FUNK-eye]

This pliosaur was discovered in 2006 in Norway. For several years, scientists called it "Predator X" because they didn't know what it was! It got its proper name in 2012.

2. *LIOPLEURODON*
[LIE-oh-PLOOR-uh-dawn]

Experts believe that *Liopleurodon* had an amazing sense of smell. It could have used the water in its nostrils to detect prey from many miles away.

KNOW WHAT?
Queensland, Australia, 2015: a farmer spraying for weeds noticed some shiny objects on the ground. He drove away at first, but felt so curious he returned. Just as well he did! He had found a jaw belonging to a young *Kronosaurus*. It measured 5.2 feet (1.6 m) long. So far, it is the most complete *Kronosaurus* jaw ever discovered.

TYLOSAURUS

LIZARD OF THE SEA

Tylosaurus [tie-lo-SAWR-us] was a type of mosasaur—a giant predatory sea lizard. It lived in the late Cretaceous period of the Mesozoic era. Its name means "knob lizard." This is because it had a rounded, bony part at the end of its top jaw. This part stuck out past its teeth, so it's a bit like it had a long nose. But you certainly wouldn't want to tease this terrifying predator about it . . .

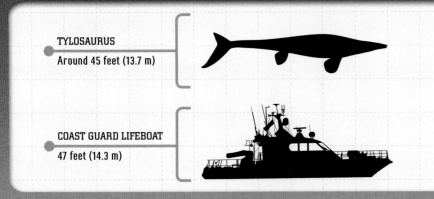

TYLOSAURUS
Around 45 feet (13.7 m)

COAST GUARD LIFEBOAT
47 feet (14.3 m)

SWIMMING LIKE AN EEL

Tylosaurus had a scaly body, four small flippers, and a large flattened tail. It swam by moving its tail from side to side, much like an eel. Its flippers were used for steering.

FAST FACT

Scientists aren't sure why *Tylosaurus* had the bony end to its jaw. Some think it may have been used as a kind of battering ram to crash into and stun its prey. It may have also been used in fights against another *Tylosaurus*.

YUM, YUM, IN TYLO'S TUM!

Tylosaurus was the apex predator of its time. While its favorite food was fish, it was also happy to munch on other sea reptiles.

CHEW YOUR FOOD! UH, OKAY, WE WON'T MAKE YOU...

Tylosaurus is related to modern snakes and monitor lizards. This includes the largest living monitor lizard—the Komodo dragon. Like a snake, *Tylosaurus* had a double-hinged jaw. This meant it could open v-e-e-ry wide! It could easily swallow some of its prey whole.

FAST FACT

In 1994, *Tylosaurus* bite marks were found on the fossil of a *Hadrosaur* (a duck-billed dinosaur.)

MEET OTHER MOSASAURS

1. *MOSASAURUS*
[MOSE-ᴀʜ-SAWR-ᴜs]

This was one of the heaviest of the mosasaurs and probably wasn't able to swim as fast as *Tylosaurus*. It weighed about 15 tons (13,608 kg.)

2. *TANIWHASAURUS*
[TAN-ɪʜ-ꜰᴀ-SAWR-ᴜs]

Fossils of this predator have been found around Japan, New Zealand, and Antarctica. It is named after the Taniwha, a dragon-like creature from Maori mythology.

KNOW WHAT?

Tylosaurus wasn't a good chewer. Its cone-shaped teeth didn't have cutting edges. But it had a secret weapon on the roof of its mouth—extra teeth! These made sure that any wiggly prey could not escape.

LIVYATAN

NOT-SO-GENTLE GIANT

We tend to think of most whales as being gentle giants, but *Livyatan* (li-VIE-ah-tan) was anything but. *Livyatan* was an ancient relative of the sperm whale—only, imagine a sperm whale with a mouth full of the largest teeth in history! Unlike its modern-day counterpart, which eat small prey, *Livyatan* attacked and ate huge sea creatures like whales . . . and may have even eaten *Megalodon*!

LIVYATAN
About 50 feet (15 m)

COAST GUARD LIFEBOAT
47 feet (14.3 m)

WHOPPER CHOPPERS

Livyatan is a fairly new discovery—its remains were first found in 2008. Scientists were searching for other whale fossils when they stumbled upon a colossal skull, complete with jaws and some teeth. The skull was about 9.8 feet (3 m) long and the teeth . . . well, you thought *Megalodon* teeth were big? *Livyatan* teeth were double the size—the largest was about the same length as a breadknife! They are among the biggest animal teeth ever.

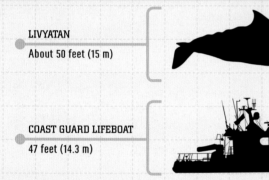

FAST FACT

The name *Livyatan* comes from the Hebrew spelling of Leviathan, a biblical sea monster.

LIVY, MEET MEG

Livyatan lived for part of the same time as Megalodon, around 12 million years ago. It was only a little smaller and ate the same kind of prey. This probably included dolphins, sharks, seals, seabirds, and sea turtles, as well as other whales. The question is: Did these two giants meet? If so, who would have won in a fight?

Scientists think *Livyatan* was smarter (its brain was probably larger), and it had bigger teeth. But *Megalodon* had a more powerful bite and wider jaws, and it was a faster swimmer.

SPERM WHALES AND LIVY

Livyatan is related to the modern sperm whale. Both are about the same size, but there are some important differences. The sperm whale dives deep underwater for its food, whereas *Livyatan* was thought to be a surface feeder. The sperm whale is also lacking in teeth—it has only small ones in its lower jaw. It really doesn't need them. It eats softer prey like squid and fish, sucking them into its mouth.

One thing *Livyatan* did have in common with the sperm whale was an organ inside its head called the spermaceti organ. This produces a wax-like liquid. It is thought it helps the sperm whale control its deep dives. *Livyatan* may have used it for echolocation (finding objects using sound waves.)

MEET OTHER PREHISTORIC WHALES

1. *BASILOSAURUS*
[BASS-ih-lo-SAWR-us]

Basilosaurus was a carnivorous whale around the same size as *Livyatan*. It lived 30—40 million years ago. Its name means "king lizard." Why? When its remains were first found, it was thought to be a reptile.

2. *CETOTHERIUM*
[SEE-toe-THEE-ree-um]

This was a whale that *Livyatan* might have dined on. It wasn't a carnivore (meat eater)—its main diet was plankton.

KNOW WHAT?
In 2016, a man walking on an Australian beach found an enormous tooth that looked very much like a *Livyatan* tooth. However, it was only about 5—6 million years old. Scientists are not yet sure if it belonged to a species of *Livyatan* or was a relative of it.

POSSIBLE LIVYATAN TEETH

PREHISTORIC SEA MONSTERS

The prehistoric seas were full of different types of predators that lived alongside sharks. There were gigantic fish; reptiles like mosasaurs [MO-zuh-SAWRZ], pliosaurs [PLY-oh-SAWRZ], ichthyosaurs [IK-thee-uh-SAWRZ], and plesiosaurs [PLEE-zee-uh-SAWRZ]; and mammals, such as whales.

FISH

Fish were the first vertebrates—animals with a backbone—on Earth. Thousands of fish species appeared during part of the Paleozoic era. This is known as the Age of Fishes. One of the fish species was the placoderm [PLAK-uh-derm]—the knights of the fish world! Their head and neck area were covered by bony armor. Some placoderms were only the length of a ruler, but others grew to a massive size. In the Mesozoic era, bony fish appeared. This included *Xiphactinus*, which was about the length of a saltwater crocodile.

REPTILES

The Mesozoic era is sometimes called the Age of Reptiles. Dinosaurs were the top predators on land, but giant reptiles ruled the sea. There were many different types. Some had giraffe-like necks, while others looked like dolphins or lizards. One of the first sea reptiles was *Nothosaurus* [NO-tho-SAWR-us]. Scientists think it hunted for prey in the sea but could also walk on land.

MAMMALS

The first mammals appeared during the time of the dinosaurs. They were tiny, furry animals. But during the Cenozoic era, mammals began to thrive and grow in size. So the whole of the Cenozoic is called the Age of Mammals. Mammals began living on the land, but some, like whales and seals, adapted to life in the sea. One of the first whales was *Ambulocetus* [AM-byoo-lo-SEE-tus]. It was the size of a sea lion. It is known as the "walking whale" because it could move on land and in the water.

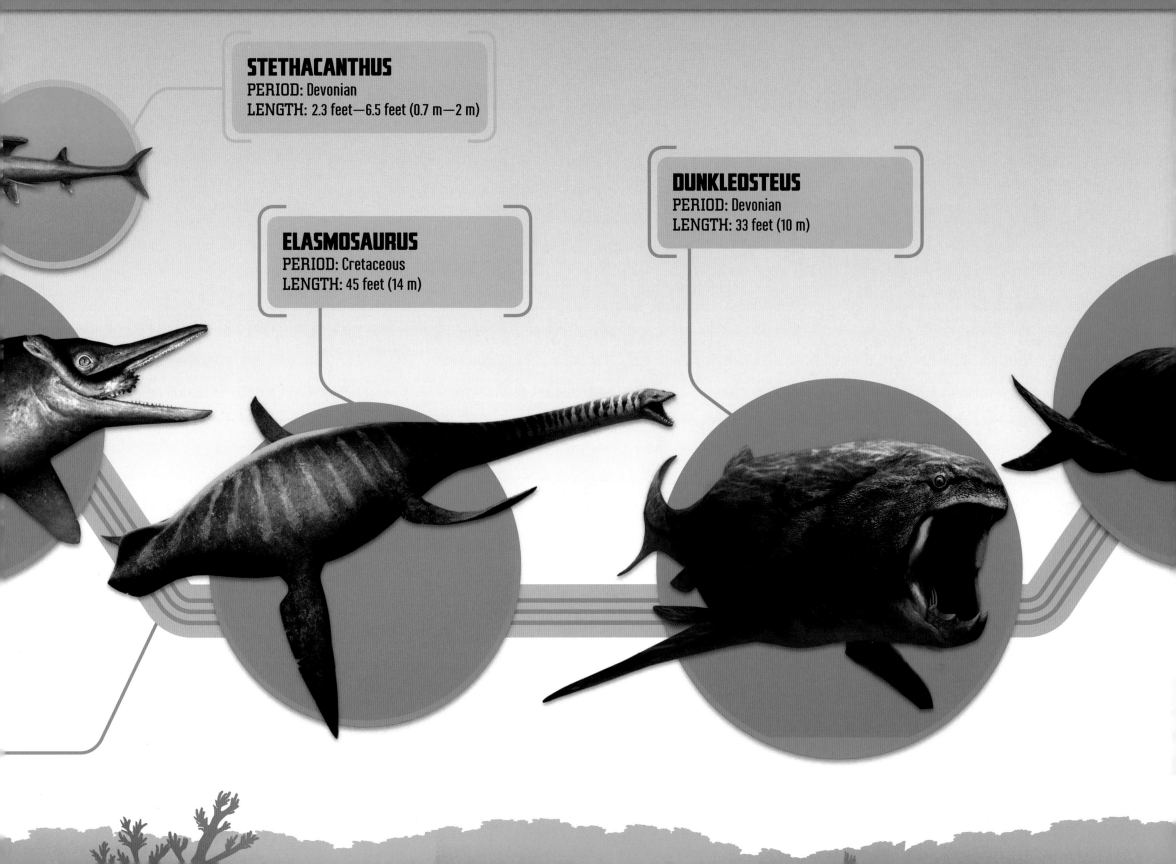

STETHACANTHUS
PERIOD: Devonian
LENGTH: 2.3 feet—6.5 feet (0.7 m—2 m)

ELASMOSAURUS
PERIOD: Cretaceous
LENGTH: 45 feet (14 m)

DUNKLEOSTEUS
PERIOD: Devonian
LENGTH: 33 feet (10 m)

MEGALODON
PERIOD: Neogene
LENGTH: 52—59 feet (15.8 m—18 m)

TEMNODONTOSAURUS
PERIOD: Jurassic
LENGTH: 39 feet (12 m)

A FEARSOME LINEUP

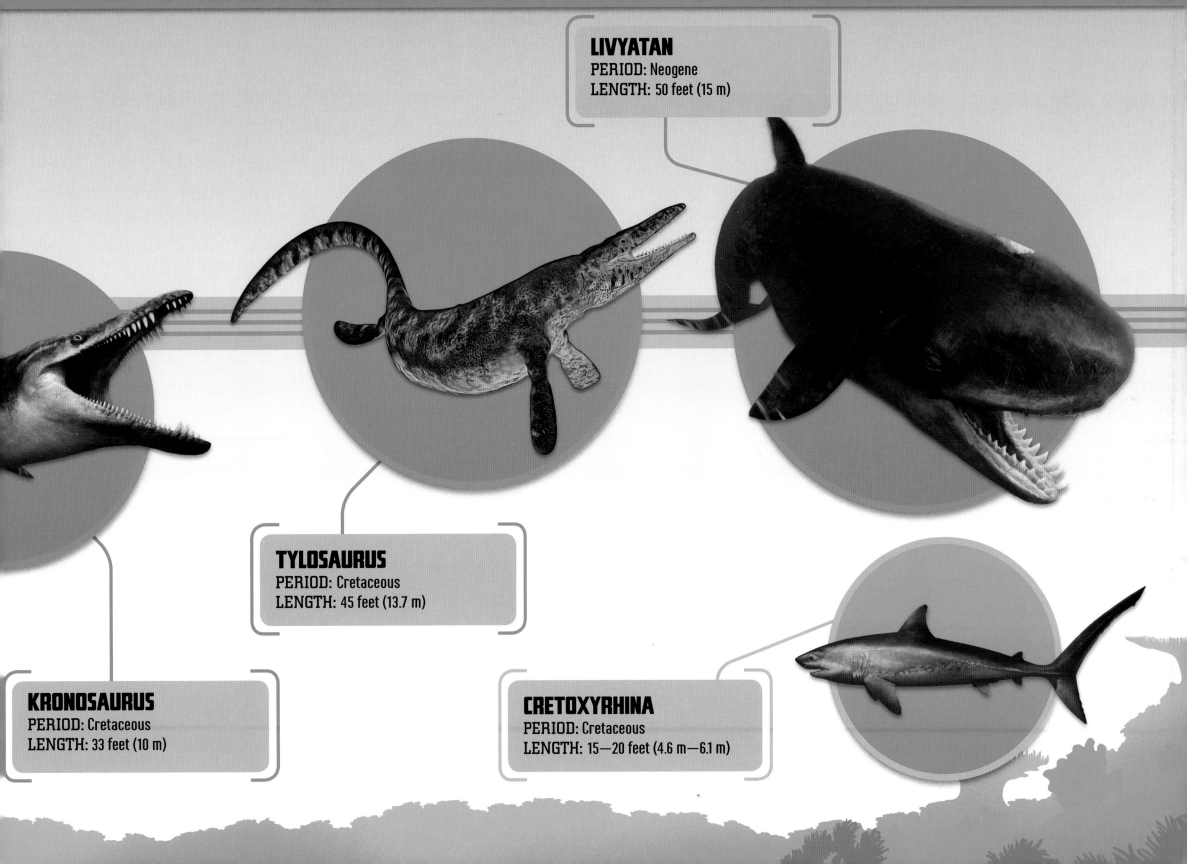

LIVYATAN
PERIOD: Neogene
LENGTH: 50 feet (15 m)

TYLOSAURUS
PERIOD: Cretaceous
LENGTH: 45 feet (13.7 m)

KRONOSAURUS
PERIOD: Cretaceous
LENGTH: 33 feet (10 m)

CRETOXYRHINA
PERIOD: Cretaceous
LENGTH: 15—20 feet (4.6 m—6.1 m)

GLOSSARY

Ammonite
An extinct type of sea mollusk with a spiral shell

Amphibian
A cold-blooded animal that lives part of its life in water and part on land

Apex predator
An animal with no natural predators within its time and place

Asteroid
A large space rock

Carnivorous
Eats meat

Cartilage
A strong, flexible connective substance in the bodies of some animals

Cenozoic
The era known as the Age of Mammals, from about 66 million years ago to the present

Cretaceous
The third geologic time period in the Mesozoic era, from 145 to 66 million years ago

Curator
Person in charge of a museum or art collection

Denticles
Tooth-like scales

Echolocation
The ability to locate objects by using sound

Era
A very long unit of time divided into shorter units called periods

Evolve
To change over many years

Extinct
A species of animal or plant that no longer exists

Fossils
Preserved body parts or traces of an animal or plant

Gastrolith
A stone swallowed by an animal to help with digesting food

Gills
A body part on an animal that allows it to breathe underwater

Ichthyosaur
An extinct marine reptile that looked like a dolphin

Invertebrate
An animal without a backbone

Jurassic
The second of three geologic time periods in the Mesozoic era, from 201 to 145 million years ago

Mammal
A type of warm-blooded vertebrate that feeds its newborn young with milk

Mesozoic
The era known as the Age of Dinosaurs, from 252 to 66 million years ago

Mosasaur
An extinct marine reptile related to monitor lizards

Paleontologist
A scientist who studies fossils to learn about the history of plant and animal life on Earth

Paleozoic
The era known as the Age of Fishes, from 541 to 252 million years ago

Placoderm
An extinct type of fish that had bony plates like armor

Planktivore
An animal that eats plankton

Plankton
Tiny plants and animals that float in the water

Plesiosaur
A long-necked prehistoric marine reptile

Pliosaur
A plesiosaur with a short neck and big head

Predator
An animal that hunts and kills other animals for food

Prehistoric
The time before written history

Prey
An animal that is hunted and eaten by predators

Reptile
A type of cold-blooded vertebrate that has scaly skin and usually lays eggs

Species
A group of animals or plants that are similar and can produce offspring

Spermaceti
A waxy substance taken from the oil in the head of a sperm whale

Triassic
The first of three geologic time periods that make up the Mesozoic era, from 252 to 201 million years ago

Vertebrae
Small bones that make up the spine

Vertebrate
An animal with a backbone

© 2018 Quarto Publishing Group USA Inc.
Produced in 2018 by becker&mayer!, an imprint of The Quarto Group, 11120 NE 33rd Place, Suite 201, Bellevue, WA 98004 USA.
www.QuartoKnows.com

17 18 19 20 21   5 4 3 2 1

ISBN: 978-0-7603-6301-0

Author: Brenda Gurr
Illustrator: R.J. Palmer
Design: Sam Dawson
Editorial: Jill Saginario
Production: Tom Miller
Product Development: Peter Schumacher

Printed, manufactured, and assembled in Shenzhen, China, 10/18.

Image credits (Images used throughout): Herschel Hoffmeyer/Shutterstock.com, katatonia82/Shutterstock.com, Warpaint/Shutterstock.com, Ase/Shutterstock.com, Quick Shot/Shutterstock.com, sittitap/Shutterstock.com, Ms Moloko/Shutterstock.com, AlexTanya/Shutterstock.com, Konstantin G/Shutterstock.com, LHF Graphics/Shutterstock.com, posscriptum/Shutterstock.com, Faviel_Raven/Shutterstock.com, Natali Snailcat/Shutterstock.com, portumen/Shutterstock.com, Michael Rosskothen/Shutterstock.com, Catmando/Shutterstock.com, Klara Viskova/Shutterstock.com, SunshineVector/Shutterstock.com, Creative Mood/Shutterstock.com,

jivacore/Shutterstock.com, Rost9/Shutterstock.com, Nebojsa Kontic/Shutterstock.com, AuntSpray/Shutterstock.com, Lefteris Papaulakis/Shutterstock.com, frantic00/Shutterstock.com, Shane Gross/Shutterstock.com

Additional credits: Devonian Sharks/PLOS.org; Helicoprian/Dmitry Bogdanov, Wikipedia Commons; Livyatan Teeth/Ghedoghedo, Wikipedia Commons; Megalodon Jaw/ Heritage Auctions, HA.com.

Special thanks to:
Michelle Johnston at KronosaurusKorner.com (Kronosaurus jaw); Mike Everhart at Oceans of Kansas Paleontology (Tylosaurus tooth), and The Royal Belgian Institute of Natural Sciences, Brussels (Megalodon vertebrae).

306042

ASSEMBLING THE SKELETON

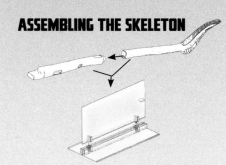

1. Attach the 2 vertebrae pieces together and assemble onto the stand.

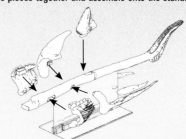

2. Insert the left gill piece into the vertebrae. Repeat with the right piece.

3. Insert the dorsal fin and 2 pectoral fins into the vertebrae. Insert the 2 pelvic fins onto the stand.

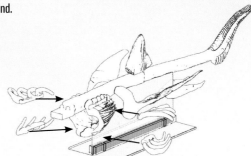

4. Insert the left rib pieces into the left gill piece. Repeat with the right pieces.

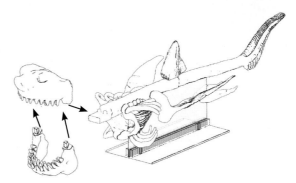

5. Attach the jaw and skull and assemble onto the vertebrae.